Punish Me Perfect

Michelle R Goodwin

BookLeaf Publishing

India | USA | UK

Made with ❤ on the BookLeaf Publishing Platform
www.bookleafpub.in
www.bookleafpub.com

Dedication

This book is for my beautiful sister, Cheri.
Who believed in me and wanted so badly for me to do
something with my poetry.
I did it sis, I love you!

And to my mother, Cat.
For teaching me the importance of pen and paper.
For always supporting me, and for being my biggest
cheerleader.

Preface

Punish Me Perfect, is truly a look into my heart, mind, and soul.

I have always had heavy emotions and when I couldn't talk about them, there was always writing. So much of what I would consider my best work, was written in times of tragedy. Years ago, all of my journals and poetry became lost. I was devastated and haven't really written much since. This book is my step forward, my promise to let go and write without fear, or regret. So, this is my introduction, there is definitely more to come. I hope these poems make you cry, laugh, scream, or just smile.

Thank you for taking the time to read it.

Acknowledgements

Thanks to Bookleaf publishing and the incredible opportunity they give to poets and writers like me.

Thank you, to my life partner and best friend, Jeba.

Thank you, to all the people who ever hurt me, and alll the boys I loved before.

And last, but not least. The hundreds of friends and strangers who have helped me in ways I can't even express.

I am forever grateful!

Preview

There is a tiny book...
Tiny, plain, and white.
Written in blood and tears,
words, that never came out right.

The pages are frayed,
The cover is battered.
Story, after story...
of how I never mattered.

If you dare to open
and see what lives inside.
You will see the truth.
the girl I try to hide.

the glimpse into my soul
the peek inside my heart
The preview of my pain
and how I fell apart.

Snake Bite

Who are you?
I'm not quite sure.
You are not the GOD,
I thought you were.

You wore a mask.
Elaborate disguise
Dug a grave for the truth.
and buried it with lies.

A beautiful distraction
Grace, honor, class.
Something left in hiding...
A snake in the grass!

Slowly, I was dying...
Poison in my veins!
No way to escape,
The prison or the chains.

Then one day it shattered.
Left me bleeding bare.
This soul inside was dying!
The heartache is so unfair!

No end to sleepless solitude,
Cold and lonely in the night.
I didn't hear the rattle,
Until I felt the bite!

Insecurity

He is perfect in my eyes,
which says to me, he is flawed.
Far beyond repair,
distant, shallow, broad.

I can see so clearly...
see right through his mask,
The mask he wears so tight.
His most binding task.

He plays it cool and calm...
put together, complete.
fearful we will all see,
How he is really obsolete.

I cannot change him,
I only know me.
And still, we both swim,
The pools of insecurity.

Cut, Copy, Paste

I strongly disagree,
With the heartache in my soul.
Is this my just reward,
For all the happiness I stole?

I barely take a breath...
My lungs collapse with fear.
is this the start of death,
Is justice finally here?

I begged for a redemption,
One I would never see.
Aiming for an image,
Of a girl I would never be.

So many years I ravaged...
So many years a waste!
Every one the same...
Cut, Copy, Paste!

Wishful Thinking

I love You badly.
Or do I?
Is this missing you,
or was it all a lie?

Am I trying to get over you,
Or grasping at straws?
Believing some great fantasy...
Of a love that never was.

Do not know which is real...
Longing or fears?
Desperate to put substance,
To all the wasted years.

So here I sit in wonder...
Cold photo in my hand.
Are you my heart's desire...
Or the supply to my demand?

He said

He said that I was boring.
He said that I was lame.
And every time he came home drunk,
He called me by her name.

He said so many sweet things,
He told them all so well!
And every time he left a mark...
He told them all I fell.

He said that I was stupid!
Told them all that I was dumb,
And every time he took a shot,
I knew just what would come.

He spoke a southern accent,
He spoke it like a saint!
Still, every time he touched me,
I felt something in me taint!

He said it was my time,
He said that I could go.
Then that day at my funeral,
He didn't even show!

Memories

They come,
They go,
They are fast,
They are slow.

Sometimes fleeting,
Sometimes lingering.

They are painful,
Joyful.
Moments from the past.

Moments, you can never make last...

Only for a moment,
before the moment is gone!

So, hold fast to the memory,
That one you treasure most.

Cause when we leave this world,
All you take...
are memories.

Loathe Me

You can smile at me...

Laugh with me.

Cry for me.

Plead to me.

Play with me.

Guide me.

Praise me.

You can call me friend,

But in the end...

I know you loathe me!

Every Time

Every time I turn around,
Someone is leaving.
Every time I hear a voice,
It is deceiving.

Every time I think it is over,
It Restarts.
Every time I get trapped,
I break more hearts.

Every time I am alone,
I think too much.
Every time things fall apart,
It is Him I clutch.

Every time I take a step,
I fall back two.
Every time I lose my way...
I run to You.

Dear Heaven

Dear Heaven,
Have you seen him?
Down here it's dark,
Far too dim.

Just over 6 foot,
Blue eyes, brown hair.
He's godda be up there...
Somewhere.

I called to him,
Late last night.
I screamed his name,
You heard it, right?

I just need to tell him
Something small.
He left without a word,
After all.

Dear Heaven,
Is he around?
Just let me see him...
I promise I wont make a sound!

I only need one smile...
Then I'll be ok,
For a while.

But if you wont give me that...
Just tell him where his daughters at.
That I am okay,
That I dont relive that harrowing day.

But if you do,
Happen to catch his eye.
Tell him that I said...
Goodbye!

Someday

"It's not goodbye, It's see ya later"
That is what you always said.
It is not goodbye,
Even when you are dead.

So here I have sat,
for fifteen long years,
Longing for later,
Choking on the tears!

"it'll get better",
That is what they all said.
So, I wait for better,
With their words in my head.

We all fell apart,
The day that you left.
Heartbreak and sorrow,
Is all you left.

Missing you,
It's just not fair!
You were supposed to raise me...
Supposed to be there!

"He's in a better place."
That is what they say...
But my soul is still broken,
Until I see you again someday.

She

She is forever chasing a life,
She cannot reach.
Bound by her mindset.
Chained by her rage.
Pacing in a labrynth...
A cage.

She is forever...
Destroying potential.
Loathing herself.
Using her sexuality.
One day she'll end up,
Just a casualty.

She is never...
Alone, she can't be.
Lost, Scared,
Cold, lonely.
Momma cries out,
"If only"!

She is never...
Happy with herself.
Makeup doesn't hide,
Smiling doesn't cure,
Got a pocketful of pain,
She must endure.

She has...
Boxed herself in,
Won't look out.
Won't look around.
Maybe she'll get it,
When they put her in the ground.

Program

Why do I try,
If the trial always fails?
Searching for some truth,
To fill these empty sails.

They are right.
I am wrong.
Lost in a game,
Where I don't belong.

Condescending and cold,
They say it as a fact.
And when the talk ends,
I'm no longer intact.

Break me down,
To build me up.
But where does it end,
When does it stop?

So here I am,
Alone in despair.
So corrupt.
So unfair.

My everything

A smile spreads across my lips,
With memories of you.
Immeasurable, Irrevocable,
Is the love I have for you!

I miss all of you!
I miss your kiss,
The sweetness of your lips!
Your subtle tenderness.

Your touch is a drug,
and the high I crave!
In it I am powerless...
I become your slave!

My body is yours,
And yours alone.
A better love,
I've never known.

You are it for me,
You make my heart sing.
You are the world to me,
My Everything!

We'll Be

You spoke the words,
I've longed to hear.
Let me be,
A listening ear.

Finally broke down,
And let me in.
A battle I thought
I'd never win.

It took so long,
To get to this place.
A mended wing,
A saving grace.

I feel so light...
My heart is free,
With hope for us,
And what we'll be!

Trick or Treat

Is it real,
Or just pretend.
These feelings,
I cannot defend.

Not sure how to trust,
The emotions inside.
Can't follow my heart,
For it has lied!

Falling in love,
Making a friend...
Where does one begin,
And the other end?

My head is dizzy.
My stomach is sick.
Is this really a treat,
Or another awful trick?

My Love

I feel the rush,
Over the riot.
I hear your voice,
Break through the quiet.

The pain melts away.
I get lost in the sound.
My love,
Somehow, I've found!

In this world
Of hate and pain,
You are the needle,
I am the vein!

Because of you,
I love me!
So much changed,
So much you'll see!

The memories we share,
I treasure so deep!
Most precious sights,
Mine to keep.

You are my world,
You are my light!
In my life full of wrongs...
You're the one I got right!

Insecure

I critique you,
Then you hate me!
The next day,
You are judging me.

It is always a game,
of tit for tat.
If I hurt you,
You will get me back.

No remorse,
No apologies.
You laugh, you stare,
You push, you tease.

Look through my eyes,
You will see,
The hidden web
Of insecurities.

Just a Dream

Don't know how I feel.
Don't know what to think.
Dare I close my eyes,
Dare I even blink?

Afraid that if I do,
All this will melt away.
Cause if this isn't real,
The pleasure cannot stay.

Dreams so vivid,
I swore they were real!
Your voice, I could hear,
Your touch, I could feel!

Yet alone I woke,
Again, in the dark.
Replaying our love,
And how I missed the mark.

Fear kept me guarded,
Pushed you miles away.
To save your heart,
You simply couldn't stay.

Now I dream of us,
Of the love we used to make.
The only thing I have to prove,
This love wasn't fake!

Monster You Made

Alone, scared...
Faded, compared!
Lost, Played...
Controlled, Afraid!
Punished, Weary...
Can't see clearly!
I am, we are...
Both gone, too far!
Come back, don't stay...
Running away!
Hate, pain...
Memories remain!
Defeated, decayed...
This monster you made!

Never Very Far

You are a drug to me,
One I cannot kick!
You must be morphine,
The way you make me itch.
The way you make me rush!

Maybe you're the Crystal...
The way you take my breath away!
The way you burn within me!
The way my judgement goes astray.

Maybe you're the needle, The stick...
The way you tear a hole in me!
You could be the cotton,
The way you make me sick!

You might be the withdrawal...
Cause without you I think I'll die!
Maybe you're the spoon,
Cause with you I get high.

I can't live with you,
Can't live without you.
So maybe you're cocaine,
Both of you are short lived,
Yet both of you remain.

I know that you're narcotic.
I can feel you in my veins!
You pierce and puncture,
Leaving scars like stains...

Til my soul is gone,
And nothing remains.

I guess you might be heroin,
Cause you make me a monster!
a fake, a fraud...
A fearless imposter!

Yes, a drug is what you are!
I know because,
The fiend for you...
Is Never Very Far!